Scribbling Grace

A KEEPSAKE DAILY PRAYER
JOURNAL FOR WOMEN

Scribbling Grace

A KEEPSAKE DAILY PRAYER JOURNAL FOR WOMEN

Jenna Parde

Get Creative 6
An imprint of Mixed Media Resources
19 West 21st Street, Suite 601
New York, NY 10010

Editor
LAUREN O'NEAL

Creative Director
IRENE LEDWITH

Designer
JENNIFER MARKSON

....

Chief Executive Officer
CAROLINE KILMER

President
ART JOINNIDES

Chairman
JAY STEIN

To my little boys. I pray you will always know and love the Lord.

978-1-68462-059-3

Manufactured in China

1 3 5 7 9 10 8 6 4 2

First Edition

Contents

How to Use This Journal

Hi! I'm so glad you have this prayer journal in your hands! I pray that it will help strengthen your relationship with Christ and deepen your prayer life. I created this journal because I found myself distracted and lost when it came to my prayer life. I was constantly returning to the same surface-level prayers and forgetting to pray over major aspects of my life, things that would cause me stress but that I never took to God, such as finances or health. This prayer journal method helped keep me engaged in my prayers and reminded me how important and powerful prayer is. I hope it does the same for you!

Each day, the journal will provide boxes for you to fill in to help you direct your daily prayer.

- Scripture: Use this box to write out a passage from your daily Bible reading or a verse that's on your mind today.

- Gratitude: List the things you're grateful for today here.

- Answered Prayers: Think back on past prayers and keep track of the ones God has answered.

- People in Need: Consider the people in your life who could use some prayer, and pray for them here.

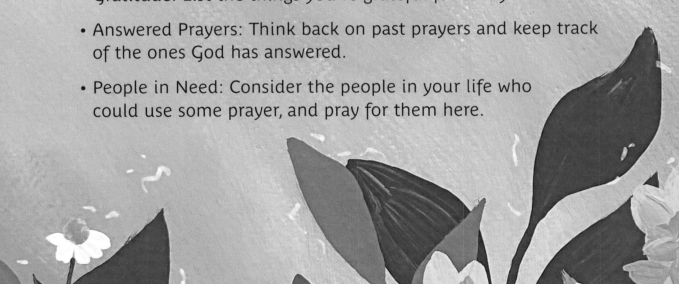

- Fears to Pass to God: What are you scared of? Give it to God here.

- Prayer: Use this box to list anything else you want to pray about.

In addition to the boxes, the journal will also provide a little something extra each day—a prayer prompt or a Bible verse to help guide your prayer.

You'll notice the journal has seven sections, each based on a different topic (relationship with God, family and friends, etc.). You'll focus on each topic for two weeks at a time. The goal is to explore the major parts of your life with God over the course of the journal, possibly diving a bit deeper into prayer than you may have before.

But ultimately, this is your journal, and you should use it however you want! If you feel like you need to pray over something different that day, do it! If you miss a day (or week or month), don't worry. Just pick it back up and dive right in again. This journal is meant to help you stay accountable to praying, but it should also be enjoyable and not cause you guilt or stress!

Praise the Lord, for he is so good! Happy praying!

Much love and many blessings,

Jenna

My relationship with God

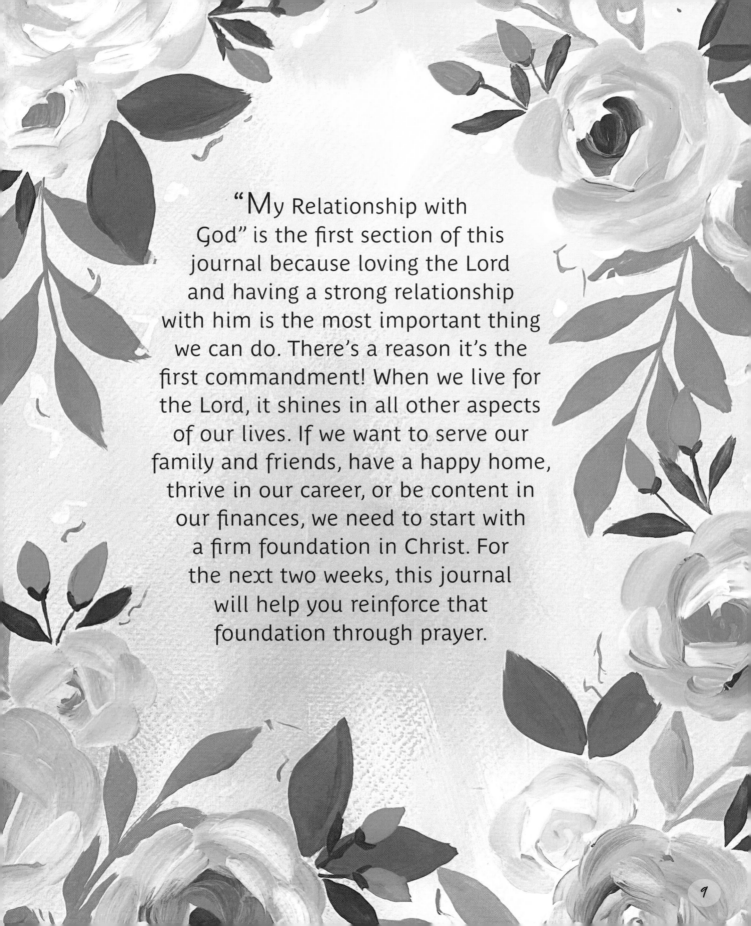

"My Relationship with God" is the first section of this journal because loving the Lord and having a strong relationship with him is the most important thing we can do. There's a reason it's the first commandment! When we live for the Lord, it shines in all other aspects of our lives. If we want to serve our family and friends, have a happy home, thrive in our career, or be content in our finances, we need to start with a firm foundation in Christ. For the next two weeks, this journal will help you reinforce that foundation through prayer.

Seek the Lord and his strength; seek his presence continually.

1 Chronicles 16:11

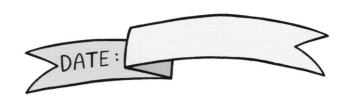

Scripture

Gratitude

Answered Prayers

People in need

Fears to pass to God

Prayer

11

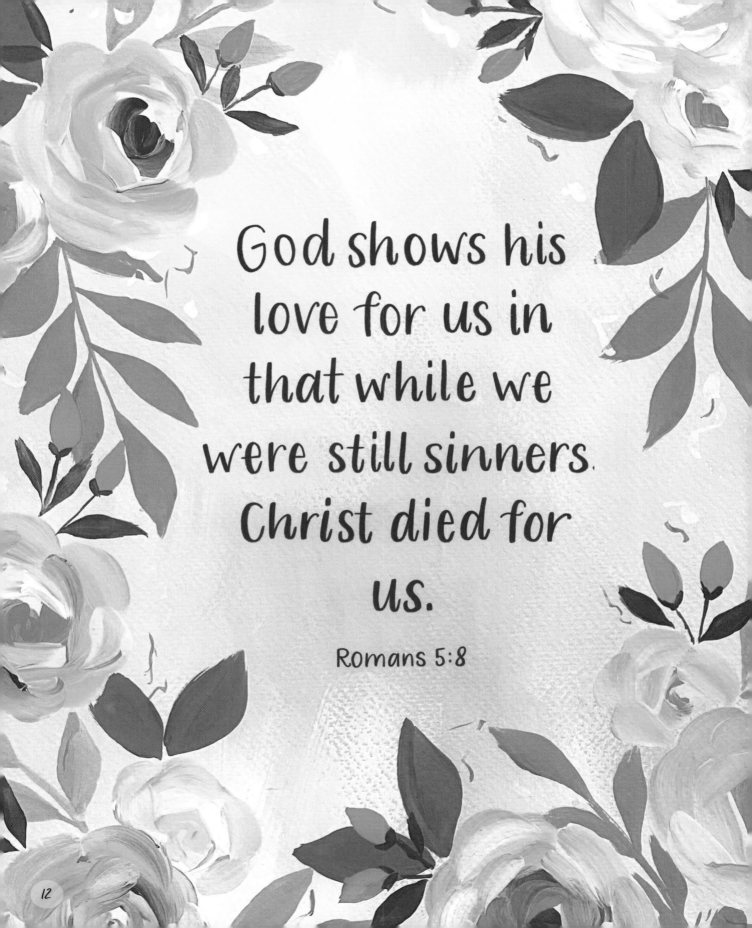

God shows his love for us in that while we were still sinners. Christ died for us.

Romans 5:8

Scripture

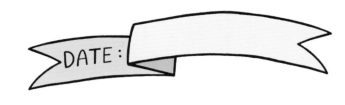
DATE:

Gratitude

Answered Prayers

People in need

Fears to pass to God

Prayer

13

Today, pray that God will open your heart to him.

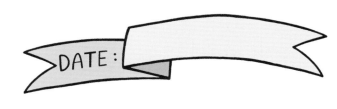

DATE:

Scripture

Gratitude

Answered Prayers

People in need

Fears to pass to God

Prayer

15

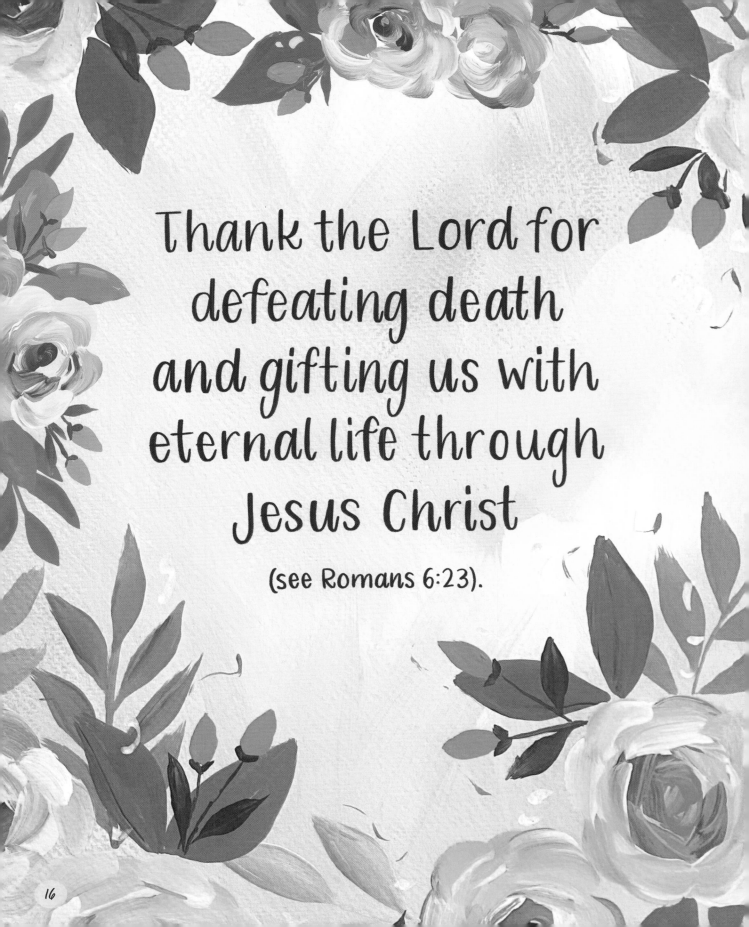

Thank the Lord for defeating death and gifting us with eternal life through Jesus Christ

(see Romans 6:23).

Scripture

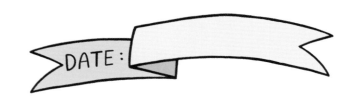
Gratitude

Answered Prayers

People in need

Fears to pass to God

Prayer

17

DATE:

Scripture

Gratitude

Answered Prayers

People in need

Fears to pass to God

Prayer

DATE:

Scripture

Gratitude

Answered Prayers

People in need

Fears to pass to God

Prayer

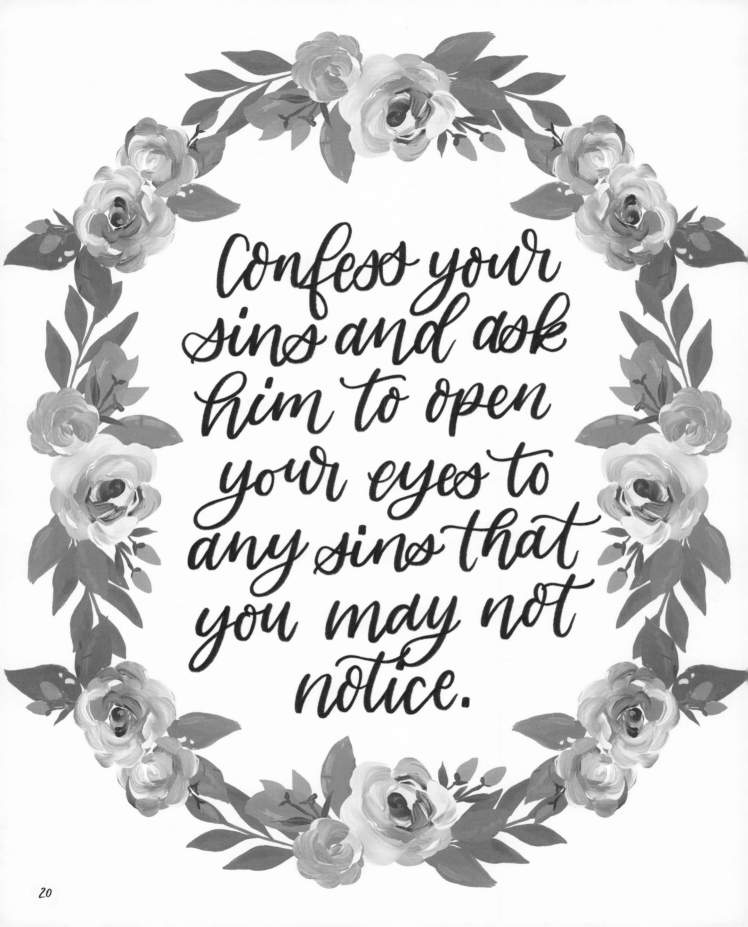

Confess your sins and ask him to open your eyes to any sins that you may not notice.

Scripture

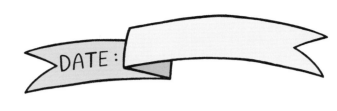

DATE:

Gratitude

Answered Prayers

People in need

Fears to pass to God

Prayer

You shall love the Lord your God with all your heart and with all your soul and with all your mind. This is the great and first commandment.

Matthew 22:37

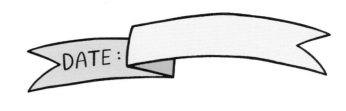
DATE:

Scripture

Gratitude

Answered Prayers

People in need

Fears to pass to God

Prayer

23

Today, pray that God fill you with the desire to seek him and read his Word.

Scripture

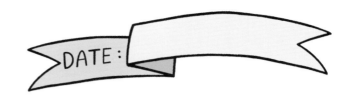

Gratitude

Answered Prayers

People in need

Fears to pass to God

Prayer

25

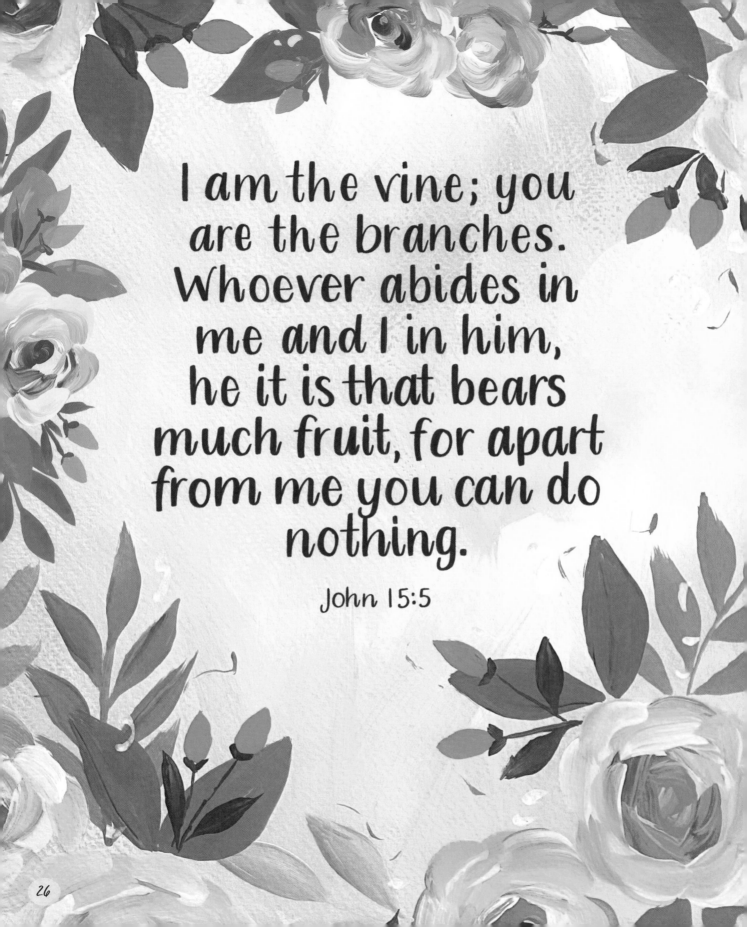

I am the vine; you are the branches. Whoever abides in me and I in him, he it is that bears much fruit, for apart from me you can do nothing.

John 15:5

Scripture

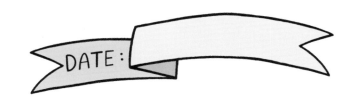

Gratitude

Answered Prayers

People in need

Fears to pass to God

Prayer

27

DATE:

Scripture

Gratitude

Answered Prayers

People in need

Fears to pass to God

Prayer

DATE:

Scripture

Gratitude

Answered Prayers

People in need

Fears to pass to God

Prayer

Ask God to use you for his purpose and to fulfill his will.

Scripture

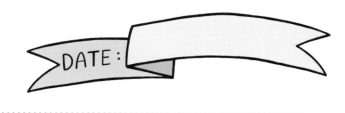

Gratitude

Answered Prayers

People in need

Fears to pass to God

Prayer

31

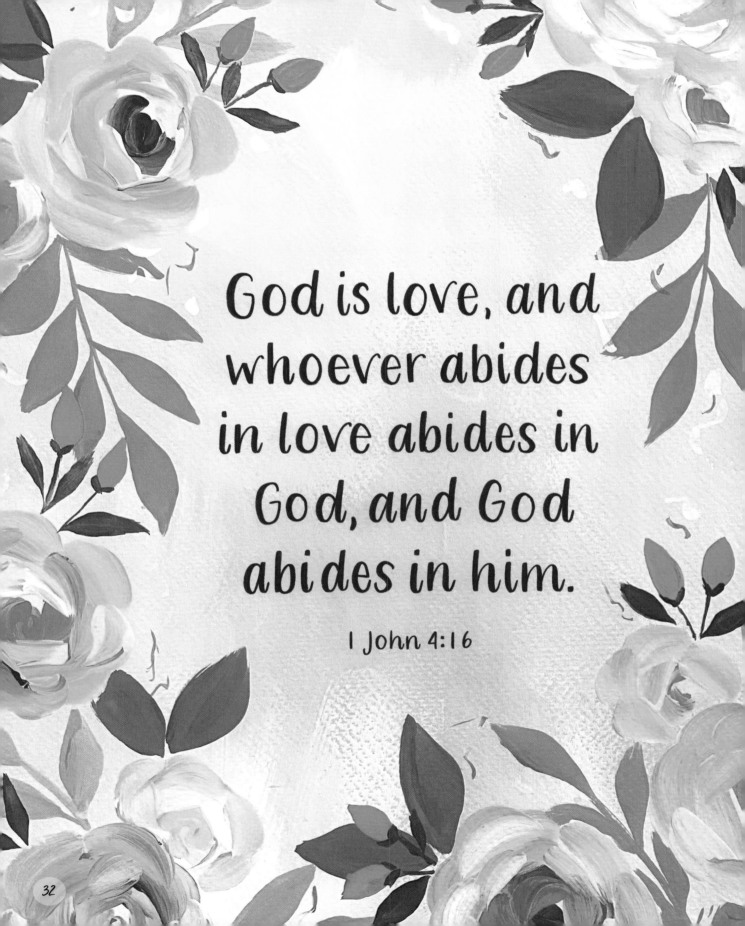

God is love, and whoever abides in love abides in God, and God abides in him.

1 John 4:16

Scripture

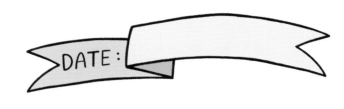
DATE:

Gratitude

Answered Prayers

People in need

Fears to pass to God

Prayer

Family and Friends

Our relationships with our family members and friends can be the greatest source of love, joy, and encouragement! However, those relationships can also be hard and messy at times. Use this section to pray over your family members and your friends for the next two weeks.

We love because he first loved us.

1 JOHN 4:19

Scripture

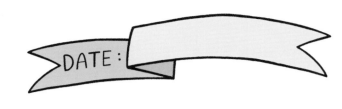

DATE:

Gratitude

Answered Prayers

People in need

Fears to pass to God

Prayer

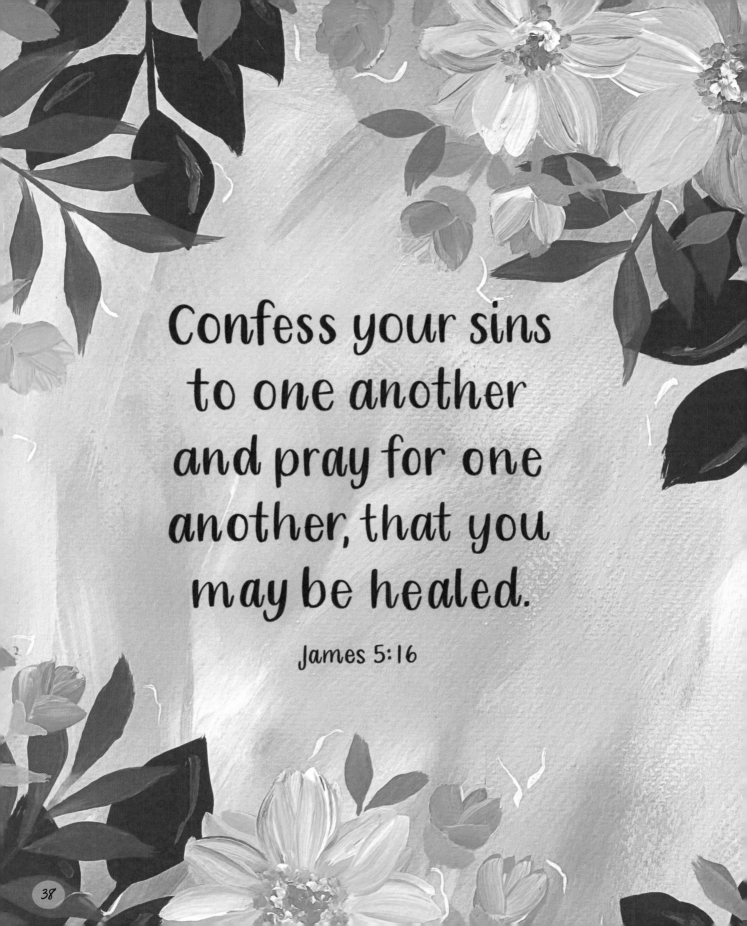

Confess your sins
to one another
and pray for one
another, that you
may be healed.

James 5:16

DATE:

Scripture

Gratitude

Answered Prayers

People in need

Fears to pass to God

Prayer

Today, pray for the health, safety, and happiness of your family members.

Scripture

Gratitude

Answered Prayers

People in need

Fears to pass to God

Prayer

Think of one or two people in your life who have specific needs or are in difficult situations right now. Pray for them today.

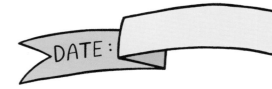

DATE:

Scripture

Gratitude

Answered Prayers

People in need

Fears to pass to God

Prayer

Scripture

Gratitude

Answered Prayers

People in need

Fears to pass to God

Prayer

DATE:

Scripture

Gratitude

Answered Prayers

People in need

Fears to pass to God

Prayer

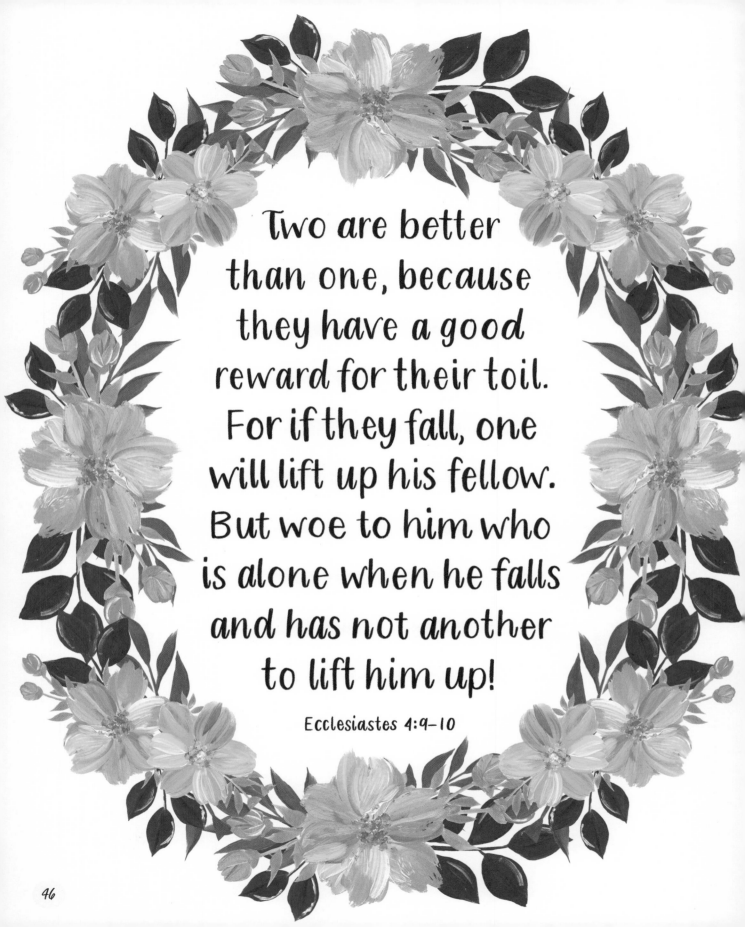

Two are better than one, because they have a good reward for their toil. For if they fall, one will lift up his fellow. But woe to him who is alone when he falls and has not another to lift him up!

Ecclesiastes 4:9–10

Scripture

Gratitude

Answered Prayers

People in need

Fears to pass to God

Prayer

Pray for your family and friends who do not know Christ, that they will come to find him, and that you can be a godly influence for them.

Scripture

Gratitude

Answered Prayers

People in need

Fears to pass to God

Prayer

Pray for your family and friends who are Christians, that their relationship with the Lord will continue to grow.

Scripture

Gratitude

Answered Prayers

People in need

Fears to pass to God

Prayer

Love one another
with brotherly affection.
Outdo one another in
showing honor.

Romans 12:10

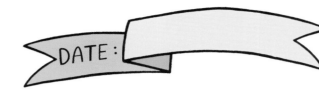
DATE:

Scripture

Gratitude

Answered Prayers

People in need

Fears to pass to God

Prayer

53

DATE:

Scripture

Gratitude

Answered Prayers

People in need

Fears to pass to God

Prayer

DATE:

Scripture

Gratitude

Answered Prayers

People in need

Fears to pass to God

Prayer

Pray
for your own
relationships with
your family and
friends to become
stronger and more
fulfilling.

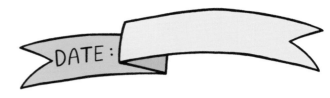
DATE:

Scripture

Gratitude

Answered Prayers

People in need

Fears to pass to God

Prayer

Pray for the
family members and
friends you may have
hurts or hang-ups with,
and ask for God's help
with forgiveness and
healing

(see Colossians 3:13).

DATE:

Scripture

Gratitude

Answered Prayers

People in need

Fears to pass to God

Prayer

59

Home and Life

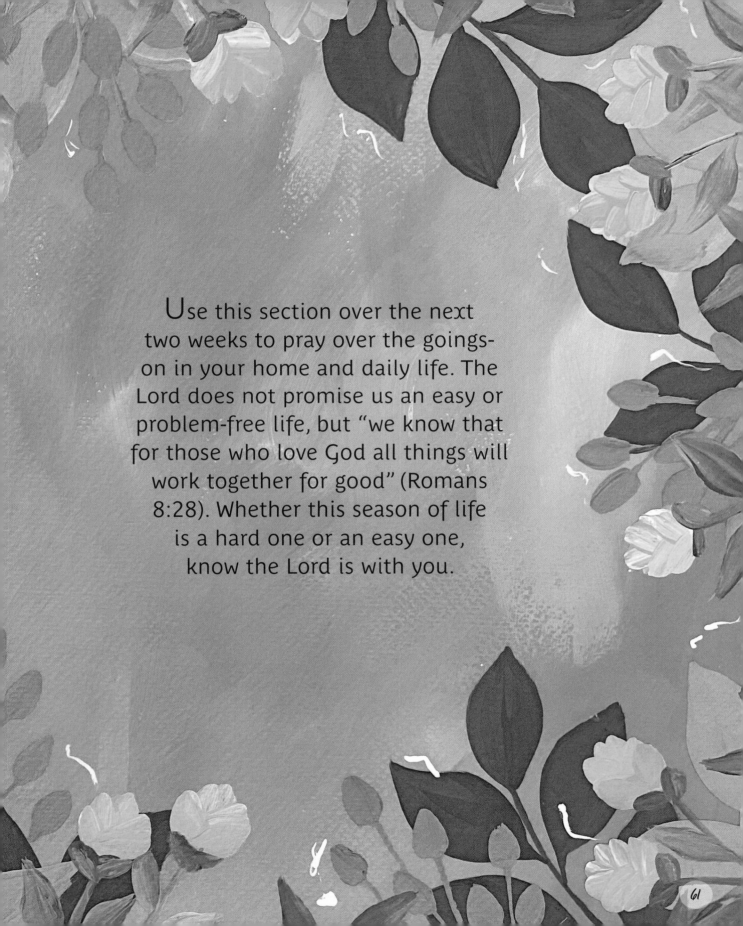

Use this section over the next two weeks to pray over the goings-on in your home and daily life. The Lord does not promise us an easy or problem-free life, but "we know that for those who love God all things will work together for good" (Romans 8:28). Whether this season of life is a hard one or an easy one, know the Lord is with you.

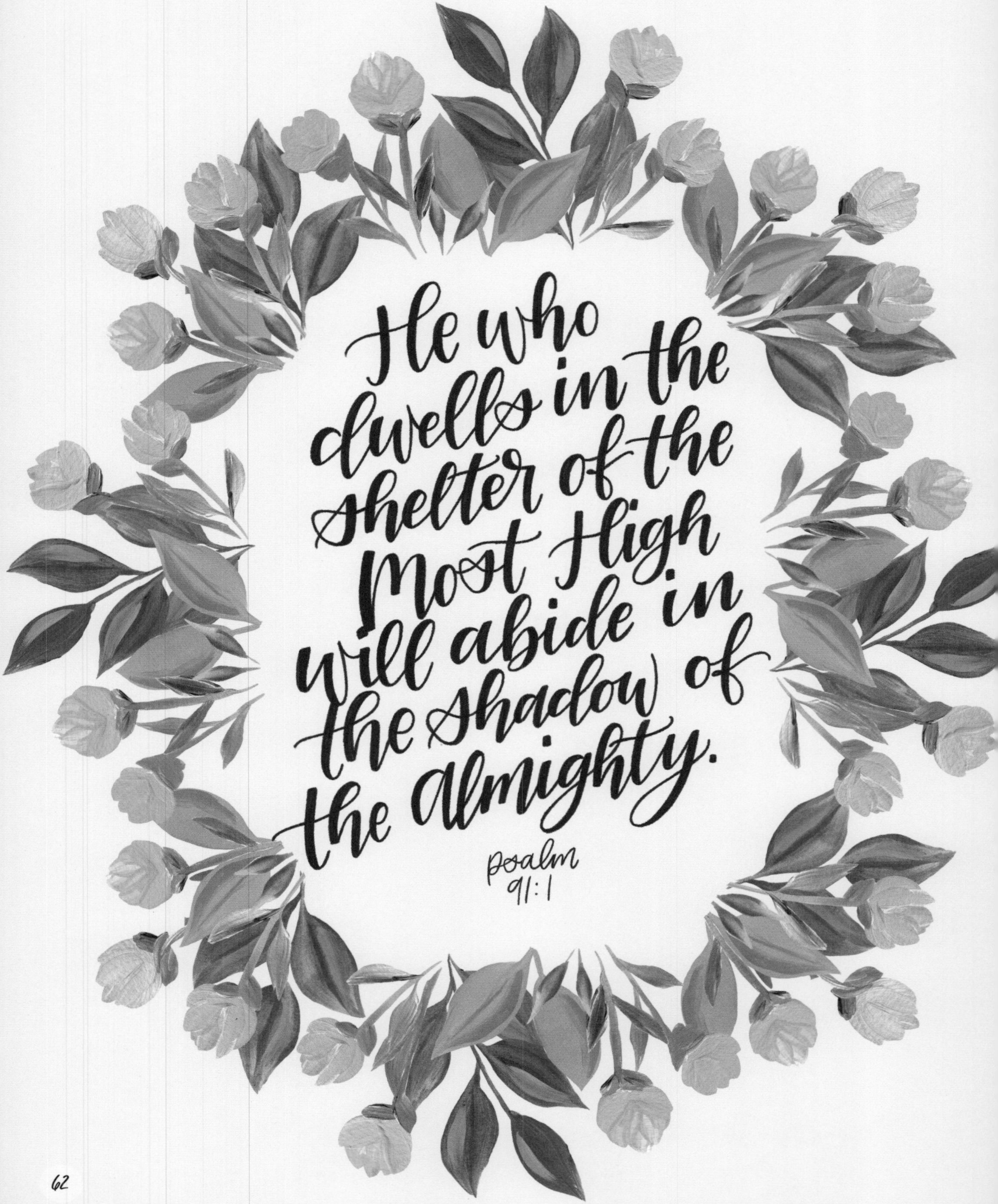

He who
dwells in the
shelter of the
Most High
will abide in
the Shadow of
the Almighty.

Psalm
91:1

Scripture

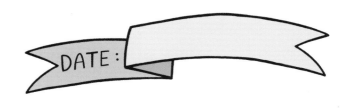

Gratitude

Answered Prayers

People in need

Fears to pass to God

Prayer

For every house is built by someone, but the builder of all things is God.

Hebrews 3:4

Scripture

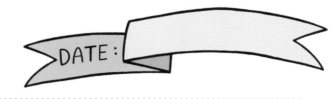

DATE:

Gratitude

Answered Prayers

People in need

Fears to pass to God

Prayer

Thank the Lord today for his provisions and the blessings in your life.

Scripture

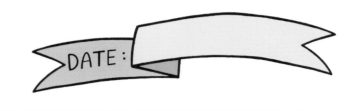

DATE:

Gratitude

Answered Prayers

People in need

Fears to pass to God

Prayer

Ask for guidance for any decisions you have to make.

Scripture

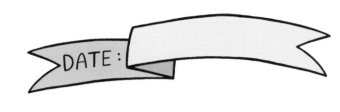

DATE:

Gratitude

Answered Prayers

People in need

Fears to pass to God

Prayer

DATE:

Scripture

Gratitude

Answered Prayers

People in need

Fears to pass to God

Prayer

DATE:

Scripture

Gratitude

Answered Prayers

People in need

Fears to pass to God

Prayer

Pray blessings upon your home and the people in it.

Scripture

Gratitude

Answered Prayers

People in need

Fears to pass to God

Prayer

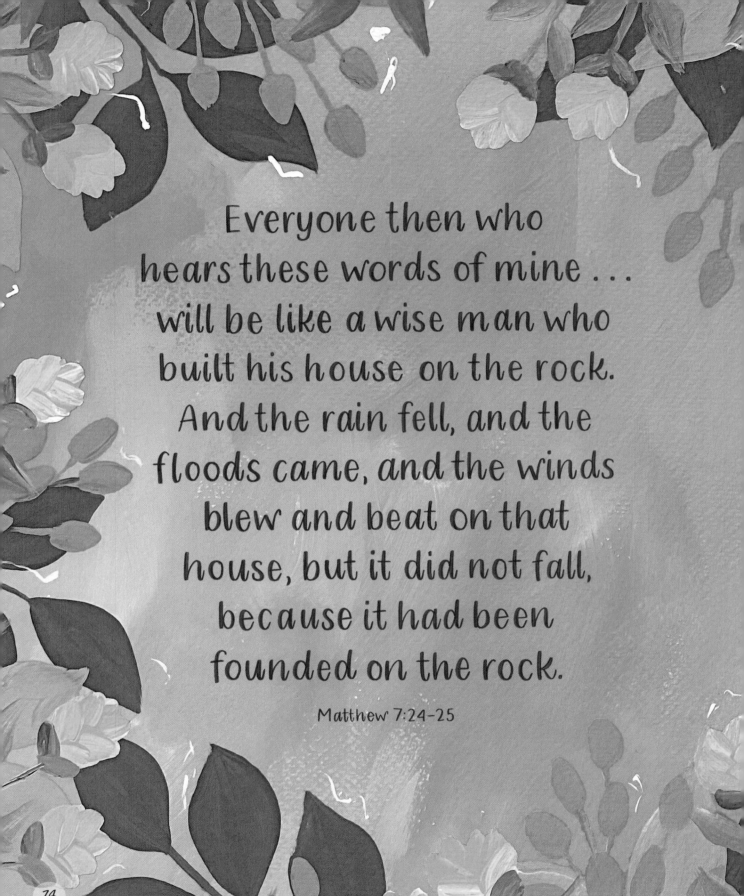

Everyone then who hears these words of mine . . . will be like a wise man who built his house on the rock. And the rain fell, and the floods came, and the winds blew and beat on that house, but it did not fall, because it had been founded on the rock.

Matthew 7:24–25

Scripture

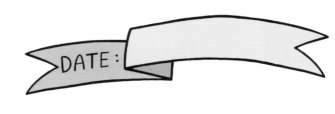

DATE:

Gratitude

Answered Prayers

People in need

Fears to pass to God

Prayer

Pray over any activities or events you have coming up.

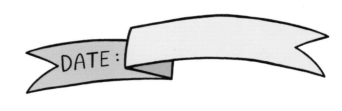
DATE:

Scripture

Gratitude

Answered Prayers

People in need

Fears to pass to God

Prayer

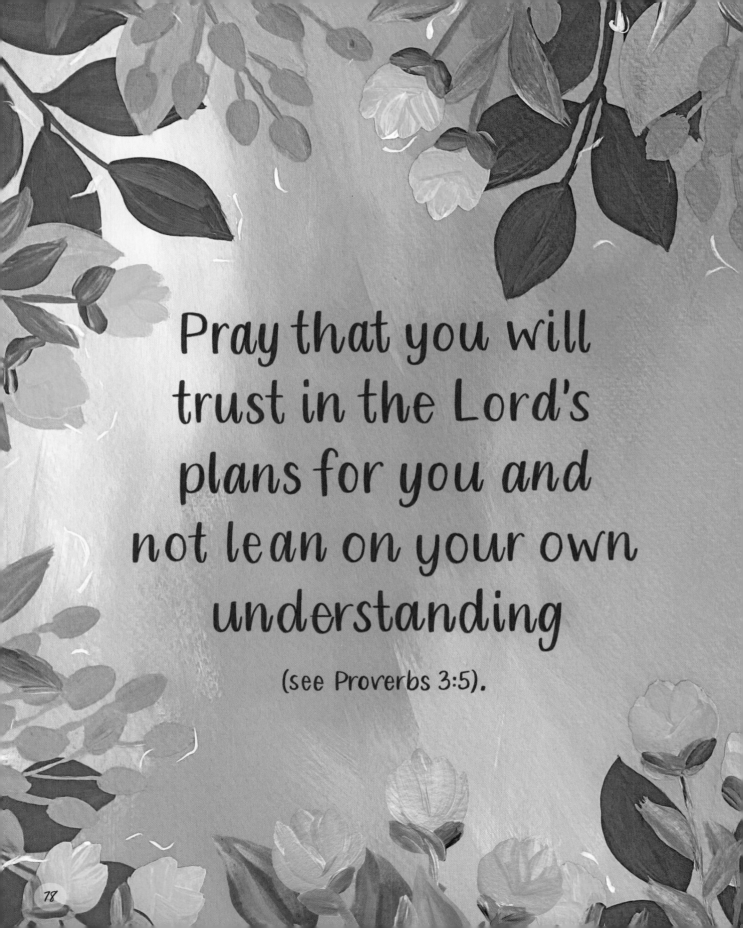

Pray that you will trust in the Lord's plans for you and not lean on your own understanding

(see Proverbs 3:5).

Scripture

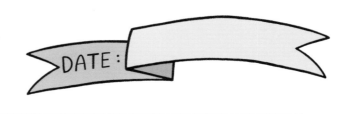

DATE:

Gratitude

Answered Prayers

People in need

Fears to pass to God

Prayer

DATE:

Scripture

Gratitude

Answered Prayers

People in need

Fears to pass to God

Prayer

DATE:

Scripture

Gratitude

Answered Prayers

People in need

Fears to pass to God

Prayer

Pray for humility, gentleness, and patience with the people and things in your life.

Scripture

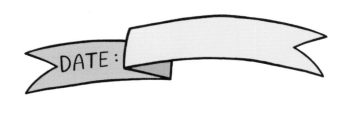
DATE:

Gratitude

Answered Prayers

People in need

Fears to pass to God

Prayer

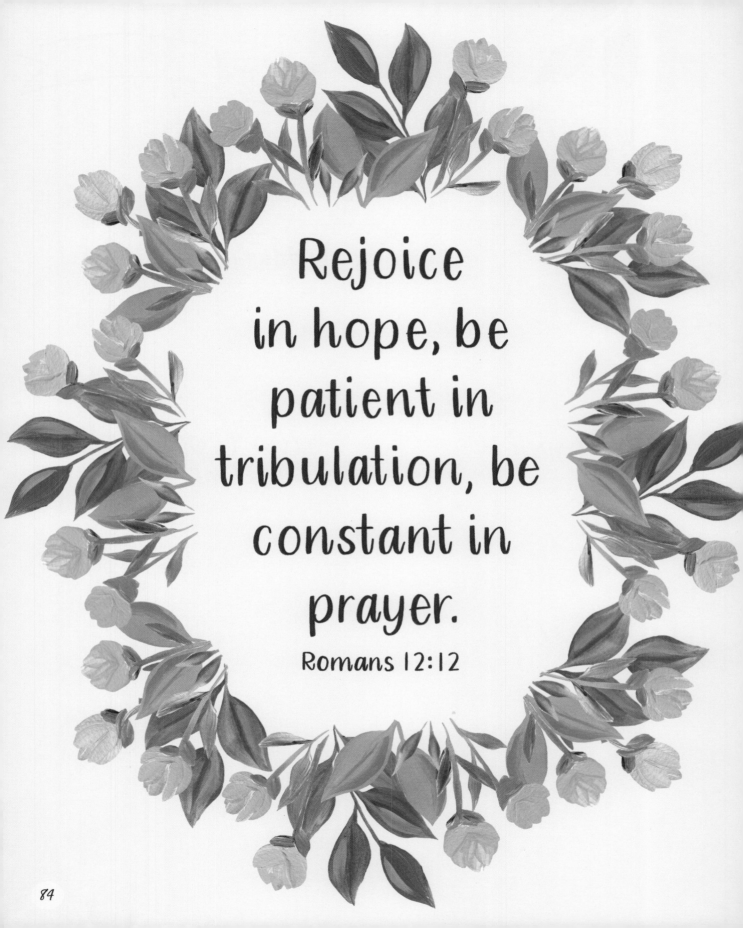

Rejoice
in hope, be
patient in
tribulation, be
constant in
prayer.
Romans 12:12

Scripture

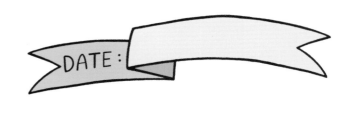

Gratitude

Answered Prayers

People in need

Fears to pass to God

Prayer

Health and Safety

Our health and safety, and
the health and safety of those
we love, can be one of the biggest
sources of anxiety in our lives.
Our bodies may fail us, and we
may not always be protected from
harm, but as Christians we have
hope that these bodies are only
temporary and that ultimately
we will find eternal joy and
peace with our Savior.

Humble yourselves therefore under the mighty hand of God so that at the proper time he may exalt you casting all your anxieties on him because he cares for you.

1 Peter 5:6-7

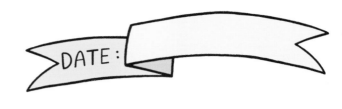

Scripture

Gratitude

Answered Prayers

People in need

Fears to pass to God

Prayer

A joyful heart is good medicine, but a crushed spirit dries up the bones.

Proverbs 17:22

Scripture

Gratitude

Answered Prayers

People in need

Fears to pass to God

Prayer

Pray for healing or continued good health in your own body.

Scripture

Gratitude

Answered Prayers

People in need

Fears to pass to God

Prayer

Pray for those you know who are going through a hard time with their health.

DATE:

Scripture

Gratitude

Answered Prayers

People in need

Fears to pass to God

Prayer

DATE:

Scripture

Gratitude

Answered Prayers

People in need

Fears to pass to God

Prayer

Scripture

Gratitude

Answered Prayers

People in need

Fears to pass to God

Prayer

Do not be anxious about anything, but in everything by prayer and supplication with thanksgiving let your requests be made known to God. And the peace of God, which surpasses all understanding, will guard your hearts and your minds in Christ Jesus.

Philippians 4:6-7

Scripture

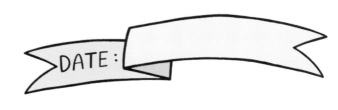

DATE:

Gratitude

Answered Prayers

People in need

Fears to pass to God

Prayer

Thank the Lord today for the gift of life and for the time we have on this earth.

Scripture

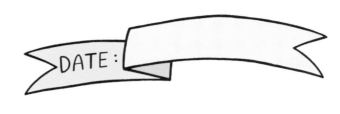

DATE:

Gratitude

Answered Prayers

People in need

Fears to pass to God

Prayer

Give
thanks for the
hope we have of a
future, pain-free,
in heaven.

Scripture

Gratitude

Answered Prayers

People in need

Fears to pass to God

Prayer

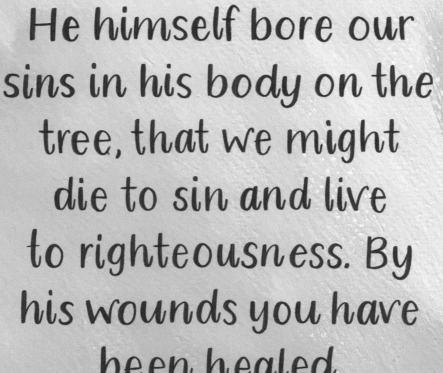

He himself bore our
sins in his body on the
tree, that we might
die to sin and live
to righteousness. By
his wounds you have
been healed.

I Peter 2:24

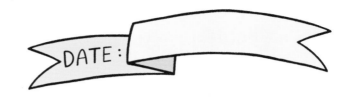

Scripture

Gratitude

Answered Prayers

People in need

Fears to pass to God

Prayer

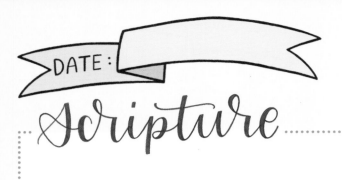

DATE:

Scripture

Gratitude

Answered Prayers

People in need

Fears to pass to God

Prayer

DATE:

Scripture

Gratitude

Answered Prayers

People in need

Fears to pass to God

Prayer

Pray that the Lord unburden you from your anxieties related to health and safety.

Scripture

Gratitude

Answered Prayers

People in need

Fears to pass to God

Prayer

Do not be anxious about your life, what you will eat or what you will drink, nor about your body, what you will put on. Is not life more than food, and the body more than clothing?

Matthew 6:25

Scripture

DATE:

Gratitude

Answered Prayers

People in need

Fears to pass to God

Prayer

Work and Career

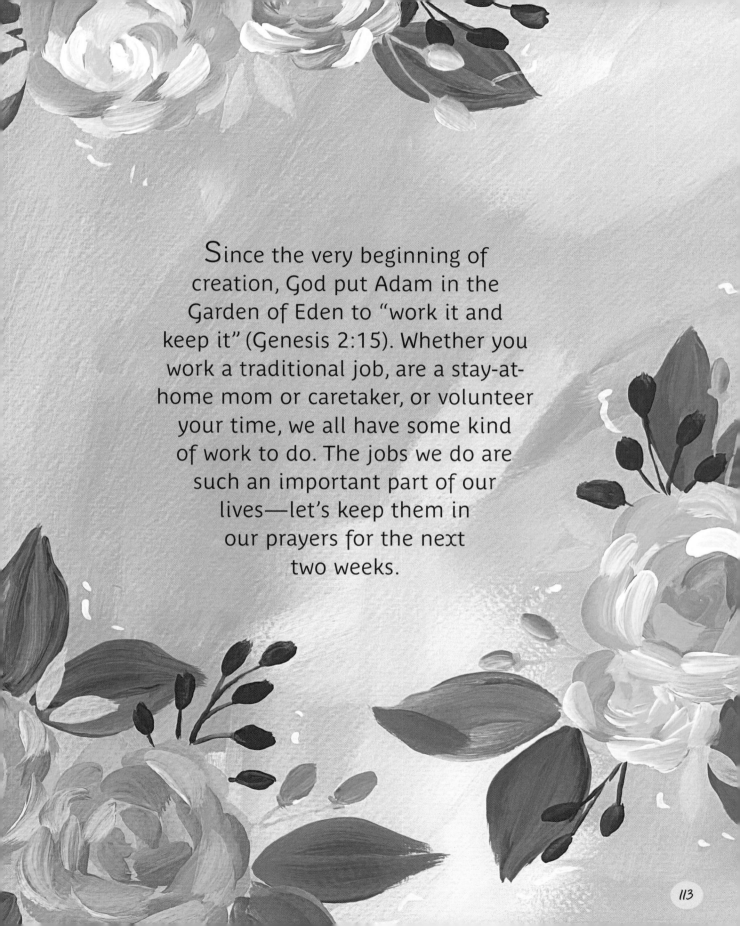

Since the very beginning of creation, God put Adam in the Garden of Eden to "work it and keep it" (Genesis 2:15). Whether you work a traditional job, are a stay-at-home mom or caretaker, or volunteer your time, we all have some kind of work to do. The jobs we do are such an important part of our lives—let's keep them in our prayers for the next two weeks.

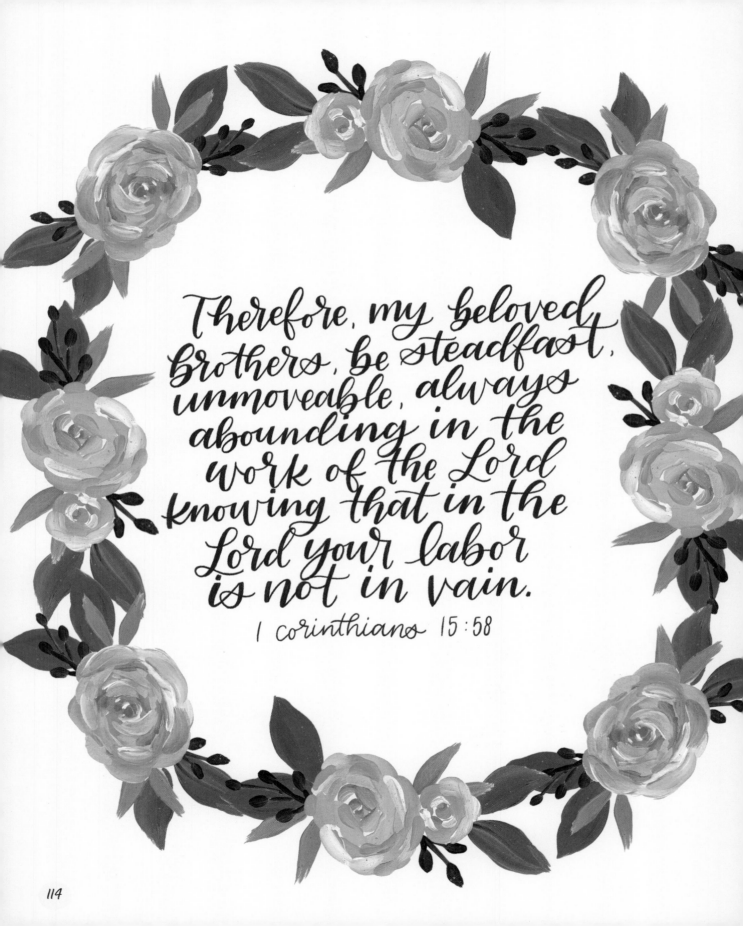

Therefore, my beloved brothers, be steadfast, unmoveable, always abounding in the work of the Lord knowing that in the Lord your labor is not in vain.

1 corinthians 15:58

Scripture

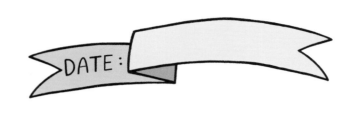

Gratitude

Answered Prayers

People in need

Fears to pass to God

Prayer

Whatever your hand
finds to do, do it
with your might.

Ecclesiastes 9:10

Scripture

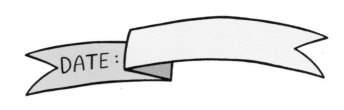

DATE :

Gratitude

Answered Prayers

People in need

Fears to pass to God

Prayer

Thank the Lord for the work you have before you.

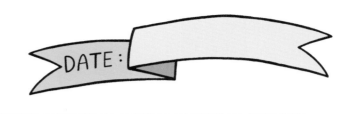

Scripture

Gratitude

Answered Prayers

People in need

Fears to pass to God

Prayer

Pray that your work, whatever it may be, will glorify God.

Scripture

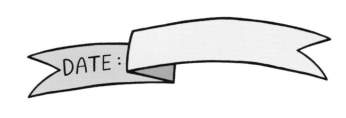
DATE:

Gratitude

Answered Prayers

People in need

Fears to pass to God

Prayer

DATE:

Scripture

Gratitude

Answered Prayers

People in need

Fears to pass to God

Prayer

DATE:

Scripture

Gratitude

Answered Prayers

People in need

Fears to pass to God

Prayer

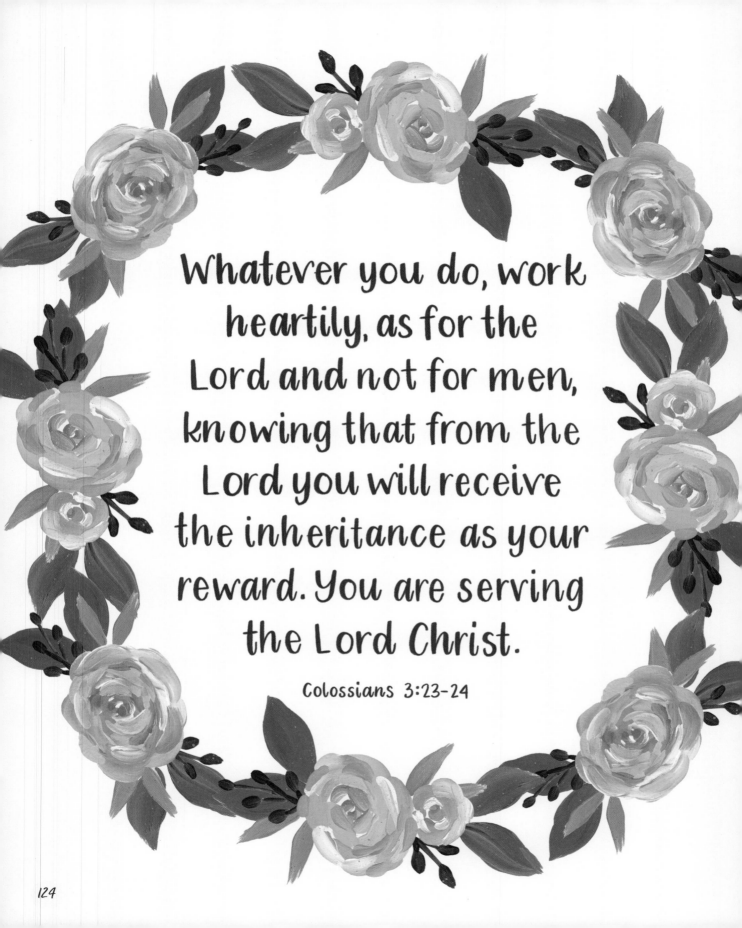

Whatever you do, work heartily, as for the Lord and not for men, knowing that from the Lord you will receive the inheritance as your reward. You are serving the Lord Christ.

Colossians 3:23-24

Scripture

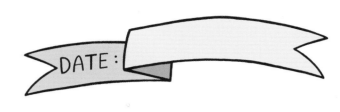

DATE:

Gratitude

Answered Prayers

People in need

Fears to pass to God

Prayer

Ask the Lord to help you "seek first the kingdom of God and his righteousness" (Matthew 6:33) rather than pursuing worldly success or the approval of man.

Scripture

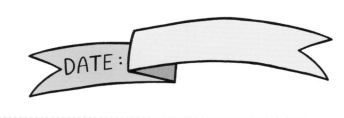

Gratitude

Answered Prayers

People in need

Fears to pass to God

Prayer

Pray for God's help as you tackle your work responsibilities today.

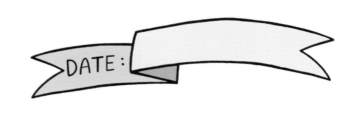

Scripture

Gratitude

Answered Prayers

People in need

Fears to pass to God

Prayer

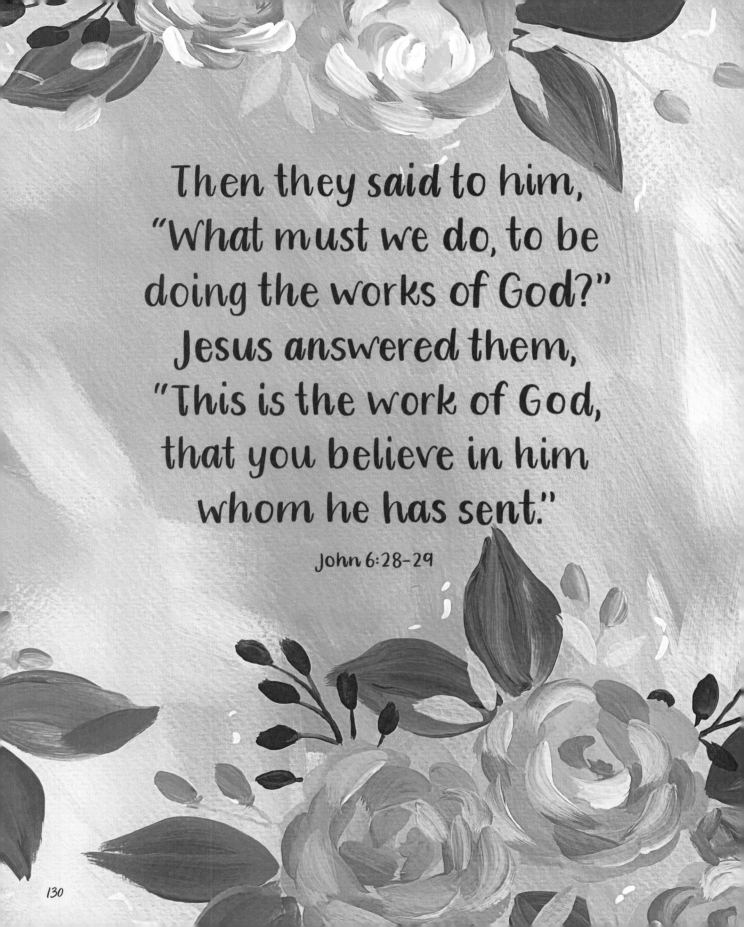

Then they said to him,
"What must we do, to be
doing the works of God?"
Jesus answered them,
"This is the work of God,
that you believe in him
whom he has sent."

John 6:28-29

Scripture

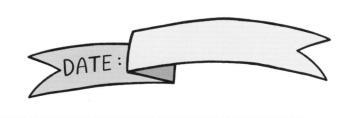

DATE:

Gratitude

Answered Prayers

People in need

Fears to pass to God

Prayer

DATE:

Scripture

Gratitude

Answered Prayers

People in need

Fears to pass to God

Prayer

DATE:

Scripture

Gratitude

Answered Prayers

People in need

Fears to pass to God

Prayer

Pray that you will be faithful to follow God's plan for your career.

Scripture

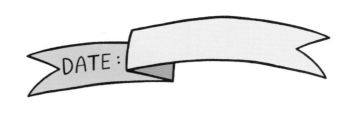

DATE:

Gratitude

Answered Prayers

People in need

Fears to pass to God

Prayer

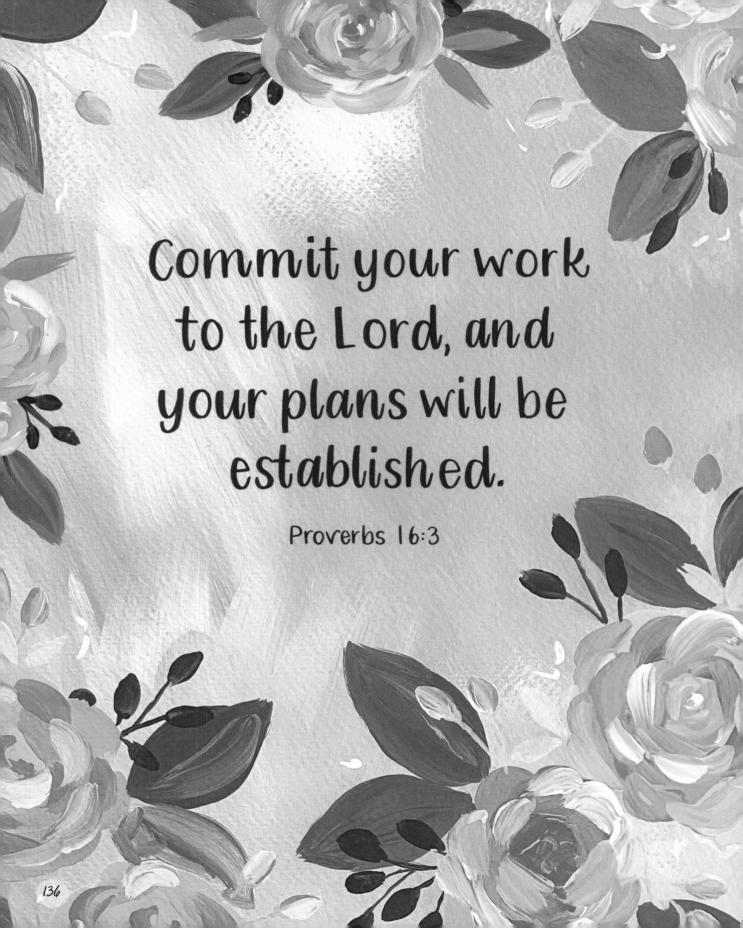

Commit your work
to the Lord, and
your plans will be
established.

Proverbs 16:3

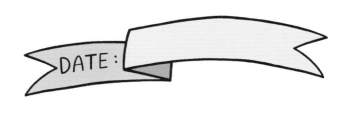
DATE:

Scripture

Gratitude

Answered Prayers

People in need

Fears to pass to God

Prayer

Finances

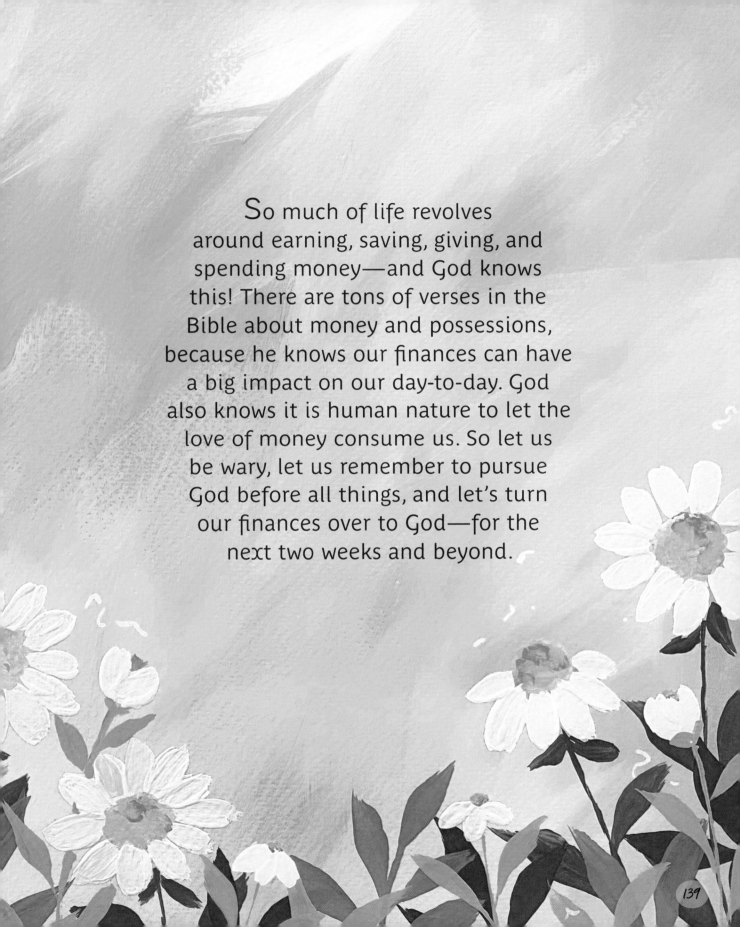

So much of life revolves around earning, saving, giving, and spending money—and God knows this! There are tons of verses in the Bible about money and possessions, because he knows our finances can have a big impact on our day-to-day. God also knows it is human nature to let the love of money consume us. So let us be wary, let us remember to pursue God before all things, and let's turn our finances over to God—for the next two weeks and beyond.

Take care and be on your guard against all covetousness, for one's life does not consist in the abundance of his possessions.

Luke 12:15

Scripture

Gratitude

Answered Prayers

People in need

Fears to pass to God

Prayer

In the day of prosperity be joyful, and in the day of adversity consider: God has made the one as well as the other.

Ecclesiastes 7:14

Scripture

Gratitude

Answered Prayers

People in need

Fears to pass to God

Prayer

Thank
the Lord for
the money and
possessions you
have been blessed
with.

Scripture

Gratitude

Answered Prayers

People in need

Fears to pass to God

Prayer

Pray that he will provide for any financial needs you, or people you know, may have.

Scripture

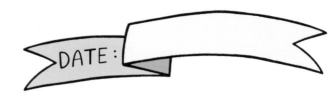

DATE:

Gratitude

Answered Prayers

People in need

Fears to pass to God

Prayer

DATE:

Scripture

Gratitude

Answered Prayers

People in need

Fears to pass to God

Prayer

DATE:

Scripture

Gratitude

Answered Prayers

People in need

Fears to pass to God

Prayer

As for the rich in this present age, charge them not to be haughty, nor to set their hopes on the uncertainty of riches, but on God, who richly provides us with everything to enjoy. They are to do good, to be rich in good works, to be generous and ready to share...so that they may take hold of that which is truly life.

1 Timothy 6:17-19

Scripture

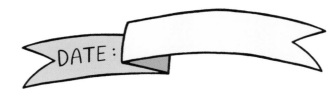

DATE:

Gratitude

Answered Prayers

People in need

Fears to pass to God

Prayer

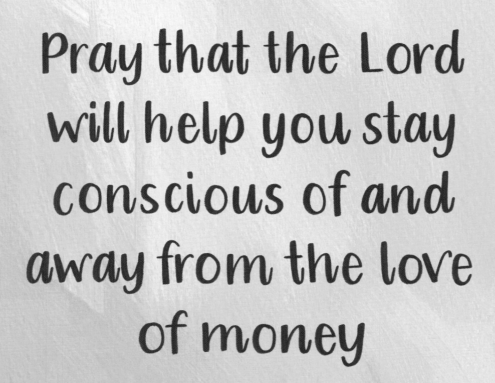

Pray that the Lord will help you stay conscious of and away from the love of money

(see Hebrews 13:5, 1 Timothy 6:10).

Scripture

 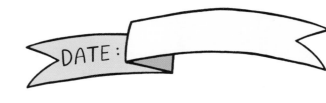
Gratitude

Answered Prayers

People in need

Fears to pass to God

Prayer

Pray
that God help
you be a good
steward of your
money.

Scripture

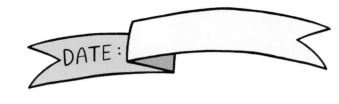

DATE:

Gratitude

Answered Prayers

People in need

Fears to pass to God

Prayer

Ask God to grow your generous heart and to show you where to donate.

Scripture

Gratitude

Answered Prayers

People in need

Fears to pass to God

Prayer

DATE:

Scripture

Gratitude

Answered Prayers

People in need

Fears to pass to God

Prayer

DATE:

Scripture

Gratitude

Answered Prayers

People in need

Fears to pass to God

Prayer

Pray that God will help you with decisions that will impact you financially.

Scripture

Gratitude

Answered Prayers

People in need

Fears to pass to God

Prayer

As for what was sown among thorns, this is the one who hears the word, but the cares of the world and the deceitfulness of riches choke the word, and it proves unfruitful.

Matthew 13:22

Scripture

DATE:

Gratitude

Answered Prayers

People in need

Fears to pass to God

Prayer

The World

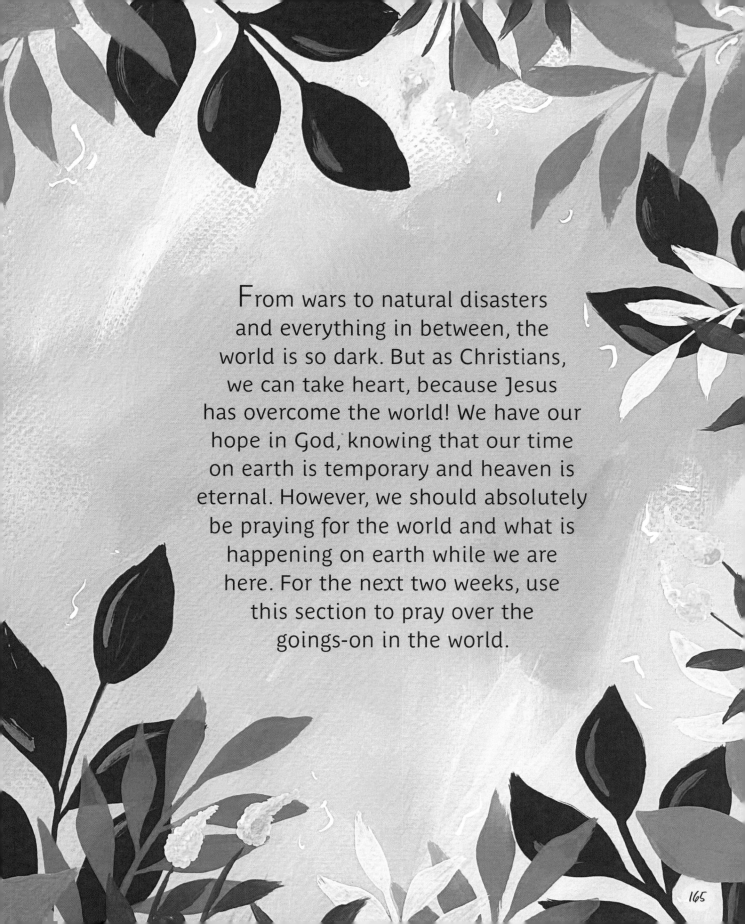

From wars to natural disasters and everything in between, the world is so dark. But as Christians, we can take heart, because Jesus has overcome the world! We have our hope in God, knowing that our time on earth is temporary and heaven is eternal. However, we should absolutely be praying for the world and what is happening on earth while we are here. For the next two weeks, use this section to pray over the goings-on in the world.

In the world you will have tribulation. But take heart, I have overcome the world.

John 16:33

Scripture

Gratitude

Answered Prayers

People in need

Fears to pass to God

Prayer

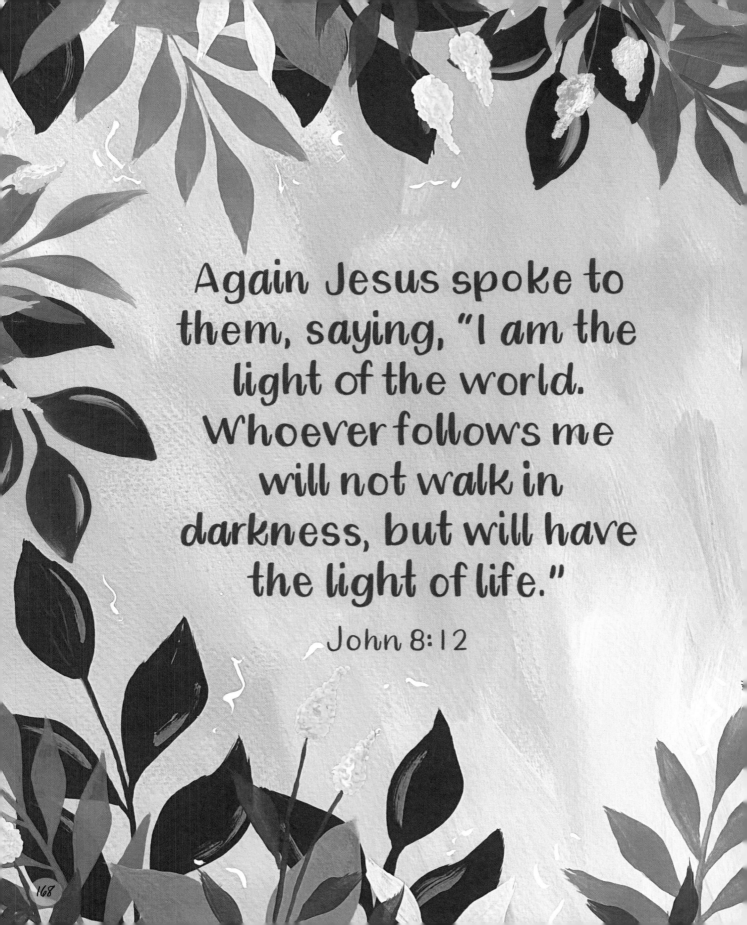

Again Jesus spoke to them, saying, "I am the light of the world. Whoever follows me will not walk in darkness, but will have the light of life."

John 8:12

Scripture

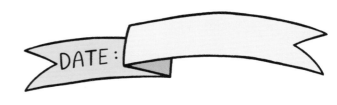
Gratitude

Answered Prayers

People in need

Fears to pass to God

Prayer

Today, pray for our world leaders, that they will make wise and good decisions.

Scripture

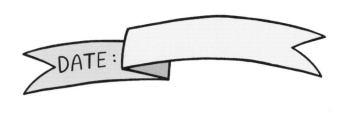
DATE:

Gratitude

Answered Prayers

People in need

Fears to pass to God

Prayer

Pray for the people affected by tragedies like famine, war, natural disasters, or other states of emergency.

Scripture

DATE:

Gratitude

Answered Prayers

People in need

Fears to pass to God

Prayer

DATE:

Scripture

Gratitude

Answered Prayers

People in need

Fears to pass to God

Prayer

DATE:

Scripture

Gratitude

Answered Prayers

People in need

Fears to pass to God

Prayer

Do not love the world or the things in the world....The world is passing away along with its desires, but whoever does the will of God abides forever.

1 John 2:15-17

Scripture

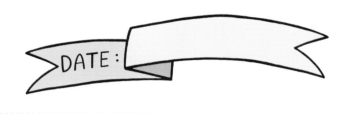

DATE:

Gratitude

Answered Prayers

People in need

Fears to pass to God

Prayer

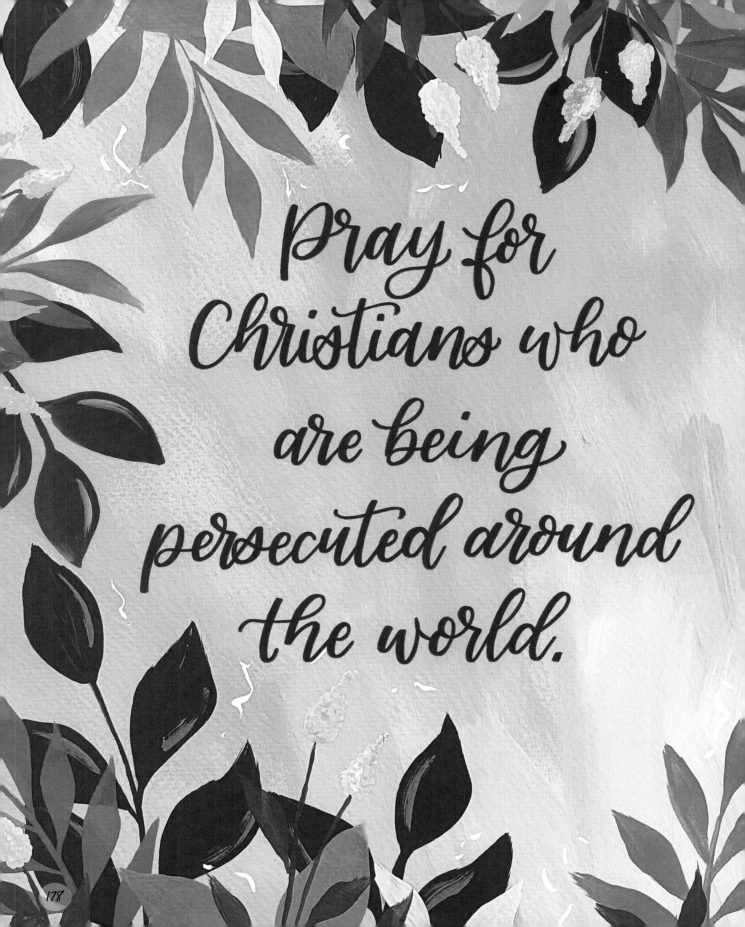

Pray for Christians who are being persecuted around the world.

Scripture

 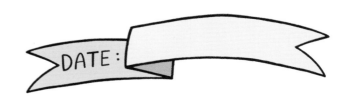
Gratitude

Answered Prayers

People in need

Fears to pass to God

Prayer

Pray for those who do not know Jesus, that they can come to know and love him.

Scripture

DATE:

Gratitude

Answered Prayers

People in need

Fears to pass to God

Prayer

Ask for God to strengthen the people who are doing his good works.

Scripture

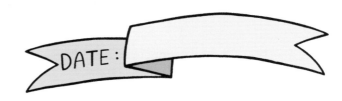

Gratitude

Answered Prayers

People in need

Fears to pass to God

Prayer

DATE:

Scripture

Gratitude

Answered Prayers

People in need

Fears to pass to God

Prayer

DATE:

Scripture

Gratitude

Answered Prayers

People in need

Fears to pass to God

Prayer

Ask the Lord
to shine his
light in the
darkness.

Scripture

DATE :

Gratitude

Answered Prayers

People in need

Fears to pass to God

Prayer

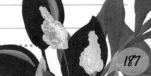

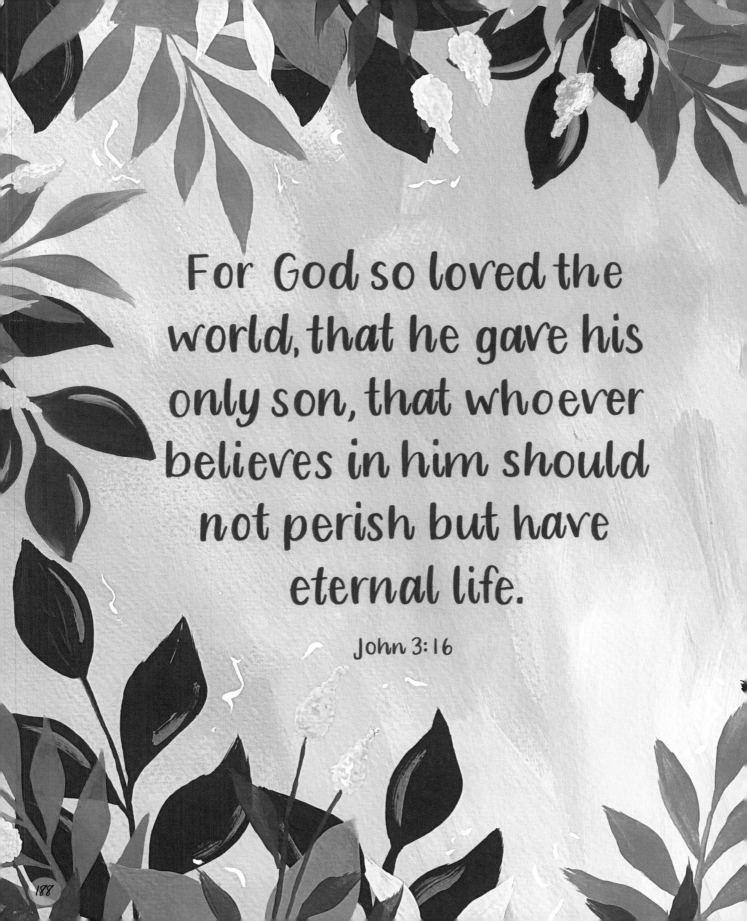

For God so loved the world, that he gave his only son, that whoever believes in him should not perish but have eternal life.

John 3:16

Scripture

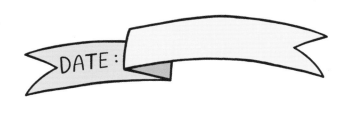
DATE:

Gratitude

Answered Prayers

People in need

Fears to pass to God

Prayer

Notes

Notes